FOR
WITH LOVE
ON

ZONDERKIDZ

Tiny Truths Little Lights Devotional

Requests for information should be addressed to:

Zonderkidz, *3900 Sparks Drive SE, Grand Rapids, Michigan 49546*

Hardcover: 978-0-310-14499-1
ePub: 978-0-310-14502-8
Audio Download: 978-0-310-14506-6

Editor: Katherine Jacobs
Art direction: Diane Mielke
Illustrations: Tim Penner

Printed in India

23 24 25 26 27 /REP/ 21 20 19 18 17 16 15 14 13 12 11 10 9 8 7 6 5 4 3 2 1

tiny truths

LITTLE LIGHTS

DEVOTIONAL

JOANNA RIVARD & TIM PENNER

TABLE OF CONTENTS

INTRODUCTION

You are a little light!

When God made you, he filled you with his light.

You are full of his love, made to care for the things he cares for and love the things he loves.

Being a little light means carrying that love with you wherever you go, shining it and sharing it with everyone you meet.

This devotional is full of ideas and possibilities to help you discover how to shine your light by:

-Loving God and your neighbors
-Standing up for what is right and fair for everyone
-Caring for creation
-Using your creativity
-Learning from the light of God in others
-Discovering the light of God in all of creation
-Finding joy in even the simplest things
-Always giving thanks to God

Even the smallest light can chase away the darkness.

Even the smallest act of love makes a difference.

You have been carefully placed in a world that needs more of God's love.

So shine bright, and
never forget who God
made you to be:
a reflection of who
he is, a little light!

WE ARE FILLED WITH LIGHT
BECAUSE YOU GIVE US LIGHT.
— PSALM 36:9 —

GOD IS LIGHT

Before the world existed, there was nothing but darkness.

And into that great darkness, God spoke:

"Let there be light!"

And there it was! The light and love of God flooded into the darkness.

It was the very first brushstroke of a beautiful painting.

Out of this God-given, God-created light, all of creation was born! Rivers and mountains, valleys and meadows, oceans and lakes, forests, flowers, and every single thing that swims, flies, and walks in the world.

Everything!

And at the very center of it all is God, the greatest light of all.

God brought light into the darkness, because that's who he is!

GOD IS LIGHT.
THERE IS NO DARKNESS IN HIM AT ALL.
— 1 JOHN 1:5 —

FILLED WITH LIGHT

In the beginning, God's light flooded into the darkness, and everything began. Creation unfolded just as God had made it to be—bursting with his light and full of his love.

When God made you, he put his light and love in you too! We are FILLED with light because God has given it to us.

God's light in you is not something you can earn, or something you could ever lose.

It's a gift!

And it's made for sharing.

So always remember who you are. You are a child of God. He has filled you with his incredible love.

You're a child of the light!

ALL OF YOU ARE CHILDREN OF THE LIGHT.
YOU ARE CHILDREN OF THE DAY.
— 1 THESSALONIANS 5:5 —

MADE IN GOD'S IMAGE

In some families you can see that people are related—they might have the same hair color, the same nose, or the same eyes. Sometimes people have the same laugh or walk the same way.

These are little clues that tell you they're from the same family.

We're not related to God in the same way, but we do carry something of him in us because we are his children. He made us to be loving, forgiving, gentle, and caring, just as he is.

When we live that way, people will see that we are a part of God's family.

When we spread and share God's light in the world, others will see what God is like because he made us to be like him.

SO GOD CREATED HUMAN BEINGS IN HIS OWN LIKENESS. HE CREATED THEM TO BE LIKE HIMSELF.

— GENESIS 1:27 —

KNOWN AND LOVED

When you were born, a new little light appeared in the world; a light that no one had ever seen before.

God created you in a way that is totally unique.

Because God made you he knows every little thing about you—the things that make you laugh, the things that scare you, and all the things you love.

He knows you better than anyone else. He sees all the possibilities you have for shining brightly.

It doesn't matter who you are, where you are, or what your life looks like today—God loves you.

God has made a world FULL of little lights. He sees each one, knows each one, and loves each one individually.

So always remember that God made you, he loves you, and he knows you.

LORD, YOU HAVE SEEN WHAT IS IN MY HEART. YOU KNOW ALL ABOUT ME.

—— PSALM 139:1 ——

NO OTHER PLACE TO BE

God's light and love are woven into the fabric of everything that he has made. You are surrounded by his goodness. It is all around you, in every little piece of our world.

God is present in his creation! You are never alone. He is always with you.

The Bible say that God wraps around us, like the arms of someone who loves us. It's comforting to know that!

There might be times when you'll worry that he's not there, or forget that he is with you.

That's normal, and God understands. But when that happens, all you have to do is look around at all he has made and be reminded that he is always with you, no matter what. Nothing can separate you from him or from his love.

YOU ARE ALL AROUND ME, BEHIND ME AND IN FRONT OF ME.

— PSALM 139:5 —

BE JOYFUL

It's much easier for you to shine your light when you know exactly who you are.

It's easier to be a light in the world when you remember who you belong to.

You belong to God. You are his, and nothing can ever change that.

When you know that you belong to God—a God who cares for you, who loves you, and is on your side—you can be joyful!

Joy happens when you understand who God is and what he has done for you. There is always something to be thankful for, always a reason for hope.

So no matter what happens, you can always find joy, because you know that you belong to God.

ALWAYS BE JOYFUL BECAUSE YOU BELONG TO THE LORD.

PHILIPPIANS 4:4

GOD'S LOVE NEVER FAILS

God is tender, kind, and gracious. He is compassionate, and never gives up on anyone, no matter what.

A love like that can never fail!

Being a little light means we carry that love in us too.

What does that kind of love look like?

It is patient with everyone, even when that isn't easy. It doesn't keep track of other people's mistakes, and when they happen, it's quick to forgive.

It doesn't get jealous, or want what belongs to someone else. This love doesn't get angry easily. It's not selfish and it doesn't need to brag. It never puts other people down, and it always protects others.

Most of all, it trusts God and is always full of hope.

Whatever happens, whatever else may come and go, God's love will last forever.

It never fails!

LOVE NEVER FAILS.
— 1 CORINTHIANS 13:8 —

WHEN IT'S DARK

It's not light all the time. Sometimes it's dark. Sometimes life feels sad or scary. But don't worry. When that happens, God is still with you.

In fact, in those moments, you can feel God's love in a new and different way.

A hug feels much more comforting when you're sad and really need it. God's love works in the same way. In the darkness and difficult times, you can feel even closer to him than when everything is bright and easy.

And the next time you find yourself in the dark, you will be able to remember that feeling.

You'll know you're not alone. You're still loved. You belong to God.

God is always there to bring you his comfort and joy.

I WAS VERY WORRIED. BUT YOUR COMFORT BROUGHT ME JOY.

— PSALM 94:19 —

THE LIGHT OF THE WORLD

Jesus is the very best example of what it is to be a light in the world.

He came to show us exactly what it looks like to share God's love and light with everyone.

He was gentle, forgiving, and kind. He cared about people who were sad, hurting, or afraid. He saw people's needs and helped them. He cared for the sick. He was friends with people who were not like him at all.

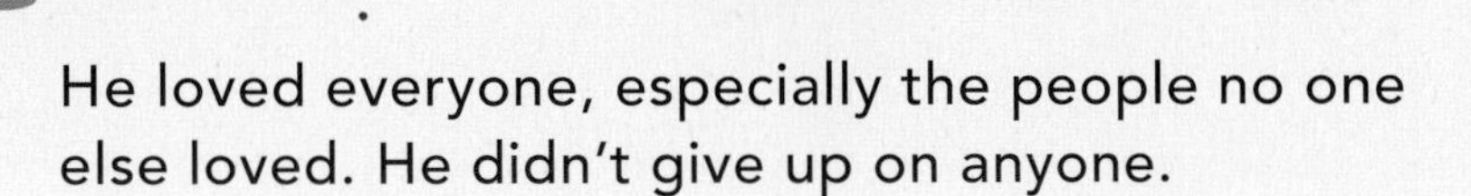

He loved everyone, especially the people no one else loved. He didn't give up on anyone.

Jesus was God's light and love in the world.

If you ever wonder what it means to be a little light, all you have to do is look at Jesus and follow his example.

YOU ARE THE CHILDREN THAT GOD DEARLY LOVES. SO FOLLOW HIS EXAMPLE. LEAD A LIFE OF LOVE, JUST AS CHRIST DID.

— EPHESIANS 5:1–2 —

EVERY LITTLE THING

When God finished creating everything, he looked at it all and said that it was VERY good!

He is a creator who loves what he has made. He cares deeply for it.

Every weird, wild, and wonderful part of creation matters to God—every creature under a rock or high in the sky, at the bottom of the ocean or the top of a mountain, hidden deep in a forest or in the park right by your house.

God sees and loves it all.

Look around and marvel at the incredible world he has given us, so full of life.

And remember, you have God's love in your heart and you were made to love the things he loves.

So let's care for God's creation as much as he does!

THE LORD IS GOOD TO ALL. HE SHOWS DEEP CONCERN FOR EVERYTHING HE HAS MADE.

— PSALM 145:9 —

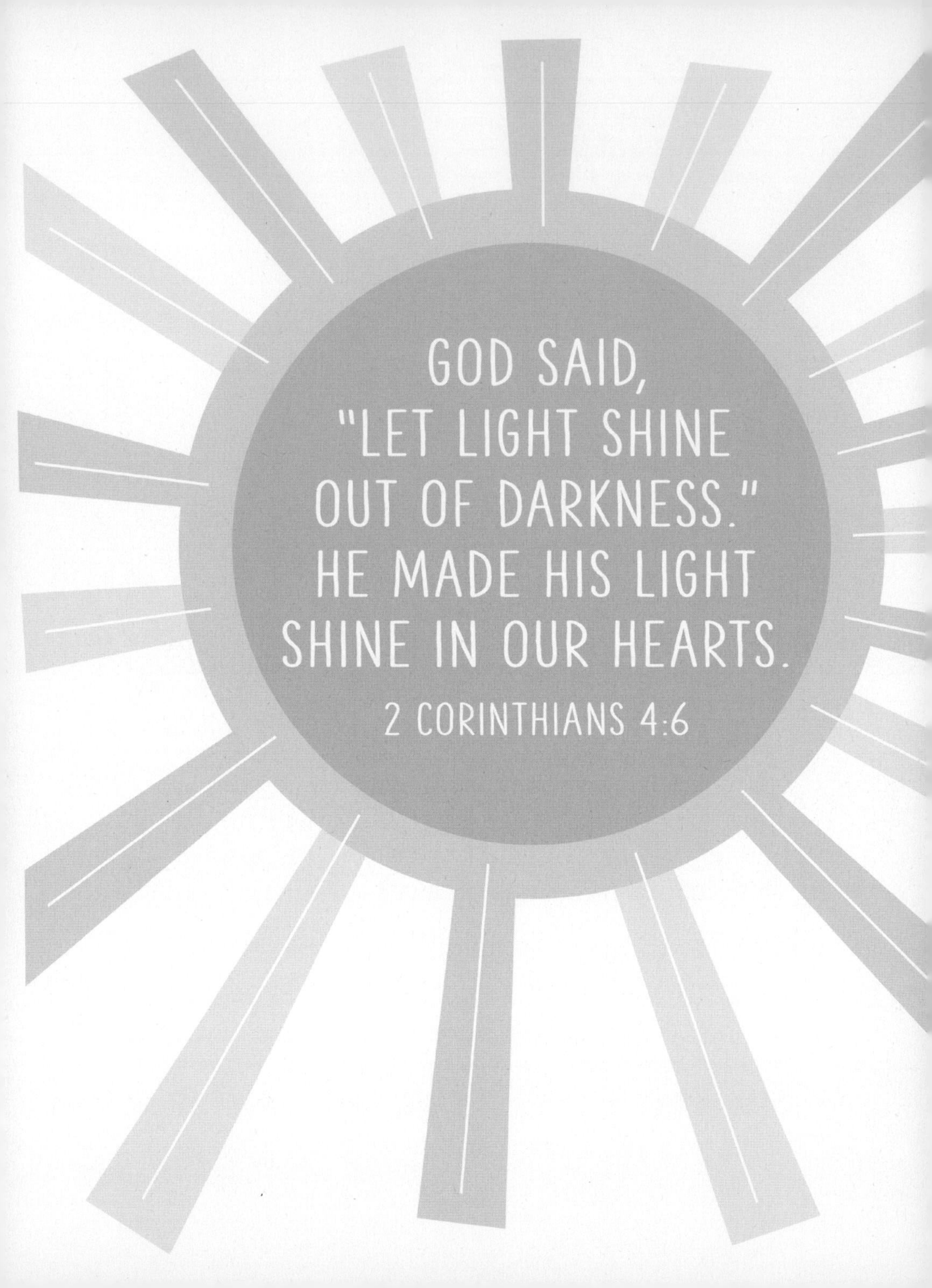
GOD SAID,
"LET LIGHT SHINE
OUT OF DARKNESS."
HE MADE HIS LIGHT
SHINE IN OUR HEARTS.
2 CORINTHIANS 4:6

GOD'S LOVE IS EVERYWHERE

God made a world full of his light and his love.

Although we don't see him, God is all around us. And so is his goodness.

Wherever you look, you will see that God's love is everywhere—you just have to pay attention.

It might be in the smile of a neighbor on the street where you live, or an elderly couple holding hands in a park.

Maybe you'll spot someone hugging a friend or bending down to greet a friendly dog. When you see someone carrying groceries for a stranger or giving up their seat on a bus, that's love.

When someone at school includes a kid who's being left out, or stands up for someone who's been treated unfairly—that's love too!

So keep your eyes open, the world is FULL of God's love!

LORD, THE EARTH IS FILLED WITH YOUR LOVE.
— PSALM 119:64 —

THE LIGHT OF GOD IN OTHERS

You are a child of God! God made you and he loves you!

Because we are all God's children, we are all loved by him and all valuable. If we forget that, we might believe that some people are more important than others. We might even make the mistake of thinking we're too important.

God sees things differently—he doesn't have favorites. He sees and loves everyone equally.

So we should too!

Everyone has something to teach you and something of God's character to show you.

Everyone has a different story, different experiences, and a different way of seeing the world. There is so much we can learn from each other when we remember that we are all made in God's image—that we all have God's light in us.

You are a gift to the people around you, and those same people—whoever they are—can be a gift to you too!

HELPING YOU FIND YOUR WAY

Life is an adventure with lots of choices to make along the way. Sometimes you need help to choose well—to see where you're going.

Some of God's best gifts are the people who help you as you grow up—parents and grandparents, aunts and uncles, neighbors and teachers.

Their experience and wisdom can be a light that shows you the way you should go.

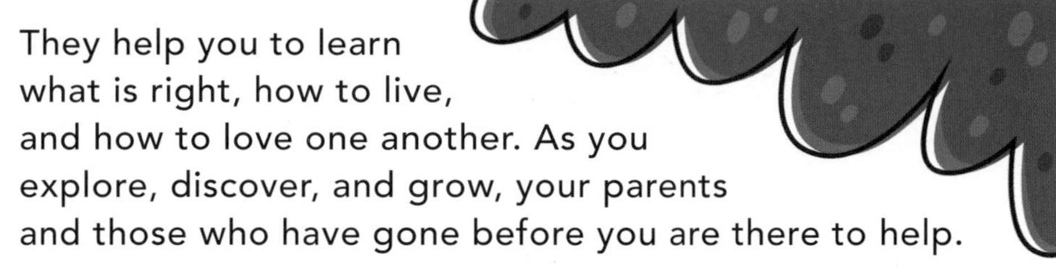

They help you to learn
what is right, how to live,
and how to love one another. As you
explore, discover, and grow, your parents
and those who have gone before you are there to help.

You don't have to find your way alone.

YOUR FATHER'S COMMAND IS LIKE A LAMP.
YOUR MOTHER'S TEACHING IS LIKE A LIGHT.
— PROVERBS 6:23 —

WE ARE ALL MAKERS

Think about all the brilliant ideas your head is full of!

Forts to play in, movies starring your dog, portraits of your friends, sketches of weird monsters, ridiculous dance moves, crazy costumes, puppet shows for your grandparents, and cakes to share! You are a maker! We all are!

That's because God is the greatest maker of all, and he made us to be like him. As his children we share his unstoppable creativity.

When you make something—whatever it is—you are reflecting God's creativity in the world, and adding to it.

You're making the world a brighter and better place by sharing what God put in you.

So never stop making what you love to make (whatever it is) because you are a child of the most incredible, imaginative, and creative maker of all!

HE IS THE MAKER OF HEAVEN AND EARTH AND THE OCEAN. HE MADE EVERYTHING IN THEM.

— PSALM 146:6 —

A LOVE THAT GROWS

Sometimes, one person's laughter can start a whole room of people laughing. It's a bit like that with the love God gives us—it grows and spreads as soon as you share it.

Usually when you share something, you have less than you had before.

But God's love doesn't work that way. In fact, the more you give it away the more of it there is. It never stops growing!

So don't hold onto it. Don't keep it for yourself.

Share it with everyone! Just imagine what would happen if we never stopped giving God's love away. Think about how far it could spread and who it could reach.

God's loving kindness can't be stopped. It never runs out. It lasts forever!

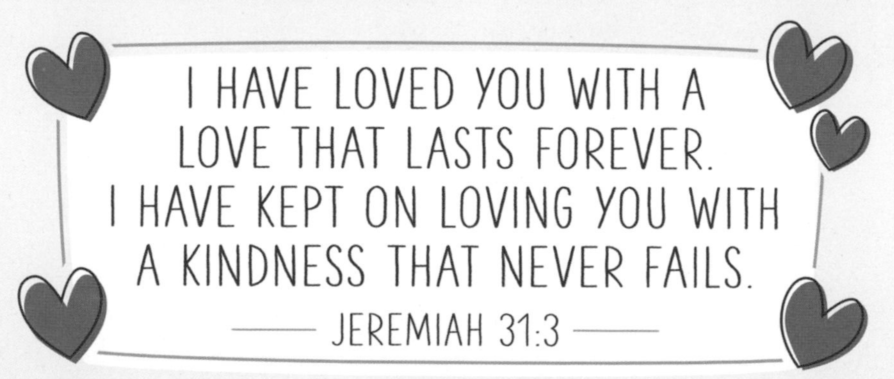

BRIGHTER TOGETHER

God made us to share our lives with each other and to shine our lights together.

A single star is bright enough to see in the dark, but when ALL the stars come out, they light up the whole night sky.

And so do we!

When we bring all of our little lights together to serve and love God, we all shine brighter.

And the brighter we shine, the easier it is for people to see the light and join us. It reminds others that they aren't alone.

It reminds us that we're not alone.

The light we share connects us to each other and it connects us all to God.

We shine the light of God brighter when we do it together!

BUT SUPPOSE WE WALK IN THE LIGHT, JUST AS HE IS IN THE LIGHT. THEN WE SHARE LIFE WITH ONE ANOTHER.

— 1 JOHN 1:7 —

FRIENDS

Friends are one of God's BEST gifts!

Friends bring light into your life in amazing ways. On the happy, bright days, they share your happiness and joy.

On the difficult, darker days, they bring you comfort and share your sadness. They can be your light when you feel overwhelmed or anxious.

Sometimes a friend is the answer to your prayer. Sometimes you will be the answer to a friend's prayer.

When you love your friends really well, you're sharing God's love with them.

God loves you through your friends and he loves your friends through you.

That brings us all closer to each other and closer to God.

MOST OF ALL, LOVE ONE ANOTHER DEEPLY.

1 PETER 4:8

EVERYONE IS WELCOME

God gives us each other—friends and family—to take care of one another and to love one another.

When we have people who love us and who we love back, it's up to us to make that love even bigger by inviting everyone to join in.

Look around and you'll see that there are a lot of people who are left out, who find themselves on the outside, or feel like they just don't belong anywhere.

Maybe there is a new person at your school, your church, or in your neighborhood.

They might look different or come from a different place. You might just spot someone who is lonely, shy, or not sure how to fit in.

You can be the person who holds out a hand or pulls up an extra chair—who invites them in. You have so much love to share.

So look for the people who feel left out, whoever they are, and welcome them in!

DON'T FORGET TO WELCOME OUTSIDERS.

— HEBREWS 13:2 —

GIVE IT AWAY

God's gifts come in many shapes and sizes. We're all good at different things. Whatever gift God has given you, he wants you to use it to serve others.

God has put so much of his creativity in you! You can always find new and exciting ways to help and serve the people around you.

Every little skill, strength, and ability you have can help someone somewhere. Every bit of kindness, generosity, and thoughtfulness makes a difference!

Think about all the things you are good at. God made you that way! So find all the ways to be a light in your home, in your school, in your neighborhood ... everywhere you go.

Use all the gifts God has given you to love and serve others. Be a gift to those around you!

EACH OF YOU HAS RECEIVED A GIFT IN ORDER TO SERVE OTHERS. YOU SHOULD USE IT FAITHFULLY.

— 1 PETER 4:10 —

GOD IS KIND

God is many things. He is powerful and strong, vast and almighty.

He is also kind—and we can be too.

Kindness isn't always something big. Sometimes it only lasts a moment. Kindness is patient rather than hurried, gracious rather than rude, gentle rather than frustrated. It's being generous instead of being selfish. It's letting someone else go first.

Kindness means caring about how we treat others.

It sends a message to the other person—I see that you are important, and that you matter.

The world we live in isn't always kind. But we can choose to be different. We can choose to carry kindness wherever we go, and to be kind to whoever we meet.

An act of kindness is perhaps the simplest, smallest way of sharing God's love in the world. It's a tiny spark of light that will always make a difference.

JOIN IN

All of creation tells God's story and, in its own way, worships God.

It's wonderful to think that the birds might be singing for joy, or that the flowers are whispering a song of praise to God. It's amazing to wonder whether the trees are shouting their worship, or whether rushing rivers are gurgling their love for their Creator.

God's creation points us to him!

Have you ever noticed that when you're outside, in nature, you feel especially peaceful, thankful, and joyful—more connected to God?

Whether you're surrounded by mountains or lakes, standing in a field, or just sitting under a tree at the park, it's incredible to imagine that creation is singing God's praise all around us! And that you can be a part of the celebration!

You just need to join in!

LET THE FIELDS AND EVERYTHING IN THEM BE GLAD ... LET ALL CREATION BE FULL OF JOY IN FRONT OF THE LORD.

— PSALM 96:12–13 —

EXPLORING THE MYSTERY

A mystery is something you can't completely understand or explain. It's a little bit secret and a little bit hidden. Mystery gets you wondering. It gets you excited and asking questions! And asking questions means that you start exploring and discovering new things.

God is FULL of mystery. There will always be things about him you won't fully understand. There'll always be more to wonder at and more to be amazed by.

There are many things that God has shown us about who he is—you can see his light and love in Jesus, his creation, and in each other. You can learn about him by reading the Bible and listening to stories of other people who love and follow him.

There'll always be more to discover!

And that's the exciting part—the more you investigate the mystery of who God is, the closer you will find yourself to him.

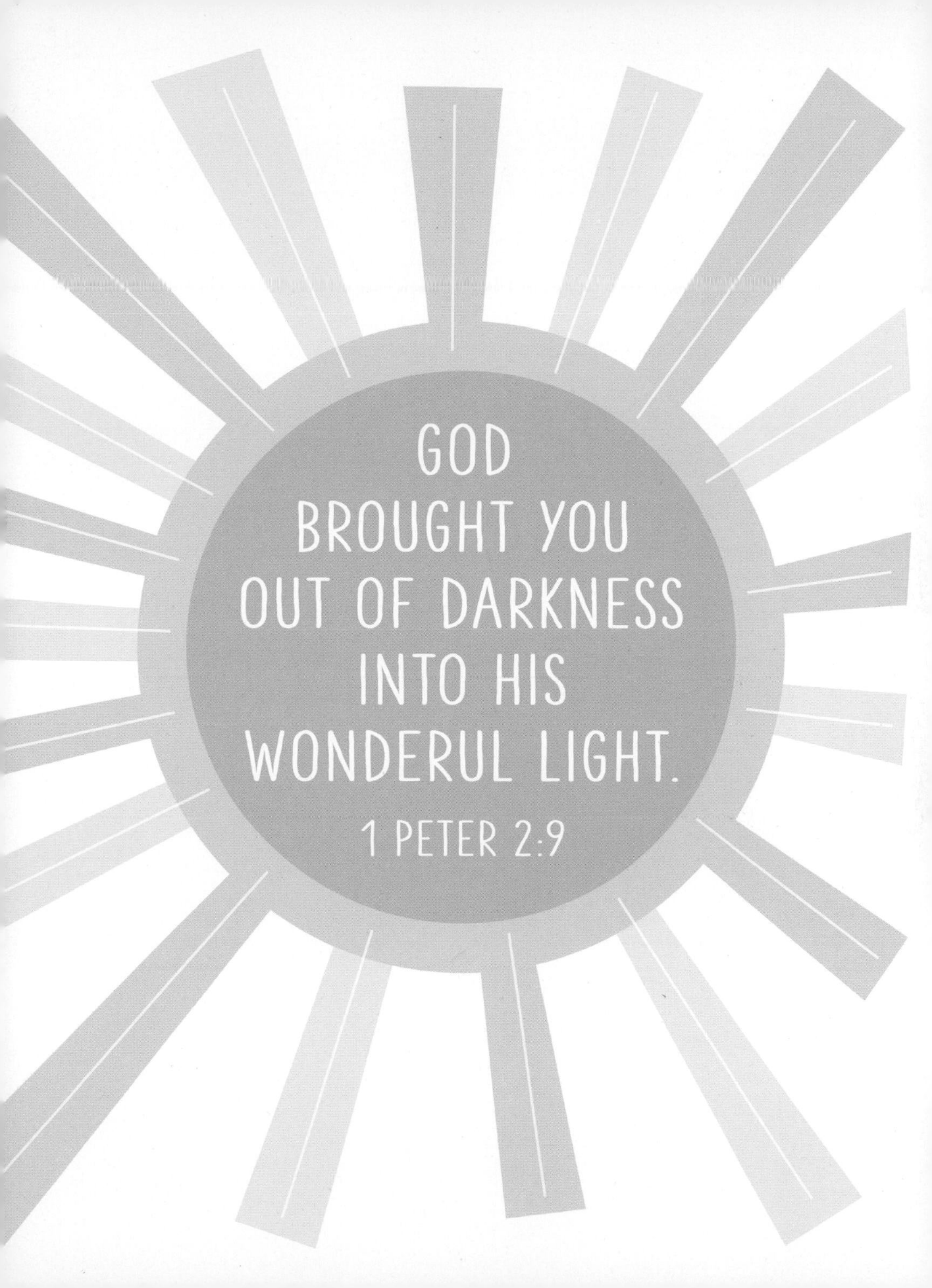
GOD
BROUGHT YOU
OUT OF DARKNESS
INTO HIS
WONDERUL LIGHT.
1 PETER 2:9

SMALL ACTS OF LOVE

There are so many different ways to shine your light and share God's love in the world.

Sometimes those opportunities are big and exciting, the kind of thing everyone will see and notice. It's easy to think that those are what matter most.

But the truth is, most of the time you just need to do the little things you can each day for the people around you. It's the small acts of kindness, the gentle words, and the helping hands that are the best way to love others and show them that they matter.

You just need to try your best to do good and share whatever you have. That's what pleases God.

If you spend too much time looking for the big things that come along from time to time, you might forget to do the simple things that are right in front of you.

So do your best to remember the small acts of love you have to share, and do them every day!

DON'T FORGET TO DO GOOD. DON'T FORGET TO SHARE WITH OTHERS. GOD IS PLEASED WITH THOSE KINDS OF OFFERINGS.

—— HEBREWS 13:16 ——

CHOOSE YOUR WORDS

God made you to love, encourage, and build others up.

There is no better way to do that than with loving and encouraging words.

Words might seem small, but they have enormous power.

Your words can remind someone that they are loved.

Words of kindness and compassion offer comfort and hope. Words have the power to heal a sad or broken heart.

You can tell someone they've done a great job.

You can use your words to express joy. You can sing and pray and say thanks for everything that God has given you!

So don't waste your words complaining, criticizing, or being unkind. Use your words for good!

Choose them wisely and use them in whatever ways you can, to bring light to others—to love and build each other up!

SAY ONLY WHAT WILL HELP TO BUILD OTHERS UP AND MEET THEIR NEEDS.

— EPHESIANS 4:29 —

TELL GOD EVERYTHING

There's nothing you can't tell God.

Happiness or sadness, excitement or anger, fear or thankfulness ... God wants to hear about it all.

When you really love someone you want to tell them everything! God wants that kind of relationship with you.

He wants you to come to him no matter what you're feeling.

When you talk to God, you feel more connected to him, you're reminded of who he is, and who you are.

You're reminded that he cares about your worries and wants to hear them.

Talking to God like this might not always change what's happening in your life, but it brings you closer to God, where you can feel his comfort. And that changes you.

When you come to God with your big feelings, and you're honest with him, it reminds you of what is true: you are a child of God, you're loved, and he is in control.

DON'T WORRY ABOUT ANYTHING. NO MATTER WHAT HAPPENS, TELL GOD ABOUT EVERYTHING.

— PHILIPPIANS 4:6 —

LOOK OUT FOR OTHERS

When you have God's light and love in you, your heart cares about the things God cares about, like making sure that everyone has what they need.

God gave us a world where there is enough for everyone, but we know that not everyone has enough.

That's because some of us have more than we need. Sometimes we take too much because we are only thinking about ourselves. Sometimes we're scared that there won't be enough for later on.

If you hold on to more than you need today because you're worried about what might happen later, someone else might not have what they need now.

The people Jesus met knew that he loved them because he saw what they needed and gladly took care of them.

You can share that same love of God when you look out for others and make sure EVERYONE has enough.

NONE OF YOU SHOULD LOOK OUT JUST FOR YOUR OWN GOOD. EACH OF YOU SHOULD ALSO LOOK OUT FOR THE GOOD OF OTHERS.

— PHILIPPIANS 2:4 —

7

DOING GOOD TOGETHER

Part of being a little light is encouraging others to shine their lights too.

Sometimes people forget that they have the light of God in them.

Maybe they have never been told.

You can be the one to remind them of who they are, and of all the good they can do in the world.

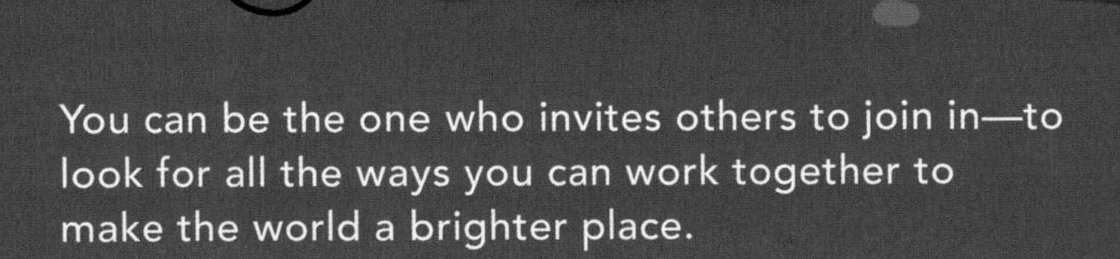

You can be the one who invites others to join in—to look for all the ways you can work together to make the world a brighter place.

So encourage others to serve more, to help more, and to love more.

Let's help one another to shine our lights!

LET US CONSIDER HOW WE CAN STIR UP ONE ANOTHER TO LOVE. LET US HELP ONE ANOTHER TO DO GOOD WORKS.

—— HEBREWS 10:24 ——

FORGIVE EVERYONE

God's love often surprises us in exciting ways.

We get to share that love in unexpected ways too!

One of the most surprising ways to use your love is to truly forgive someone when they hurt you.

You can't choose how other people treat you, but you can always choose how you respond. So when someone hurts you, what will you do with that hurt?

Will you throw it back at the person who hurt you? That will only hurt them back.

Will you hold on to it, and carry it around? It will only grow, get heavier, and wear you out.

OR will you choose to simply set it down; to forgive?

When you choose to forgive someone, it creates a new beginning—not just for the other person, but for you as well.

Forgiveness is good for EVERYONE!

MAKE SURE THAT NO ONE PAYS BACK ONE WRONG ACT WITH ANOTHER. INSTEAD, ALWAYS TRY TO DO WHAT IS GOOD ... FOR EVERYONE ELSE.

— 1 THESSALONIANS 5:15 —

LOVE YOUR NEIGHBOR

The Bible has lots to teach us about being a light in the world, but Jesus said the most important thing is simply loving God and loving your neighbor. But who is your neighbor?

Your neighbors are all the people whose lives brush against yours every day. Some you know very well, and some you simply pass at the bus stop or in the grocery store. Some offer you help when you need it and others may need your help. Some will be easy to love, and some might not.

Whoever they are, God wants you to love and care for them ALL! Every person you meet is a child of God and deserving of love.

Every single day is a new opportunity to bring God's light to your neighbors. So bring your light to everyone you meet and fill your neighborhood with God's love!

LOVE THE LORD YOUR GOD WITH ALL YOUR HEART ...
... AND LOVE YOUR NEIGHBOR AS YOU LOVE YOURSELF.
— LUKE 10:27 —

STAYING CONNECTED

God loves it when you work with him to bring more light into the world—when you're full of ideas for sharing his love and full of excitement at all there is to do.

But it's important to remember that all the strength and energy you have to shine your light comes from God. He gives it to you. So if you want to partner with God, you also need to spend some quiet time with him.

When you sit quietly with God, it reminds you that he is in control of everything. It reminds you that you are loved. It reminds you that whatever strength you have to do good in the world, whatever love you have to share, all comes from him.

In those quiet moments you find all the strength and energy and love that you need, because all of it comes from God.

THE POWER TO DO WHAT
WE DO COMES FROM GOD.
— 2 CORINTHIANS 3:5 —

GOD'S LOVE NEVER CHANGES

God IS love. And he loves you with a love that NEVER changes—no matter what.

The love that God has for you today started before anything else even existed.

We see that same love woven through all the stories in the Bible that make up the one big story of God's love for us.

We see it in Jesus, who was God's love and light to the world.

And ALL of that love is the same love that God placed in you, so carefully, when he made you—the love you have to share when you shine your light.

God's love is older than time and bigger and more wonderful than we could ever possibly imagine.

But one thing we do know is that no matter who we are or what we do, nothing can separate us from God's love.

God is good and he is faithful. His love never changes!

GIVE THANKS TO THE LORD, BECAUSE HE IS GOOD. HIS FAITHFUL LOVE CONTINUES FOREVER.

— 1 CHRONICLES 16:34 —

CARRY EACH OTHER'S BURDENS

We all need a little help from time to time, when things are difficult.

Don't forget that one of the ways God helps us, and sometimes answers our prayers, is through the people he's given us.

The Bible reminds us that we should always try to help carry one another's burdens (a burden is something that is heavy to carry).

When two people carry something together it's easier. Sometimes we need a whole crowd around us to carry something especially big.

We all have days when we need help with something heavy that's troubling us. Maybe it's a problem that needs fixing, or we just feel sad. On those days it's a comfort to know that there is help nearby.

God gives us each other to help one another.

When you help someone carry something they're struggling with, you shine a little extra light into the darkness.

CARRY ONE ANOTHER'S HEAVY LOADS.

— GALATIANS 6:2 —

WHAT REALLY MATTERS

There is far more joy in giving things away than in holding on to them.

No matter how much you have, it's always easy to want more. You might think it will make you happier. You might think it will make you seem more important.

You might even make the mistake of thinking that WHO you are is connected to WHAT you have.

But that's not how God measures our importance.

What matters most is how loved we are by God, and how well we love the people around us.

So be careful not to put all your energy into wanting and getting more for yourself.

Instead, put everything you have into sharing with others and loving the people around you.

That's what really matters!

"BE ON YOUR GUARD AGAINST WANTING TO HAVE MORE AND MORE THINGS. LIFE IS NOT MADE UP OF HOW MUCH A PERSON HAS."

— LUKE 12:15 —

DO YOUR BEST

You don't have to be perfect to be a little light!

You just need to shine wherever you are.

When Jesus came to show us how to live, the friends he chose to be closest to him—his disciples—were definitely not perfect. He didn't wait until they were, or tell them to go away and come back when they had everything worked out. He knew that they would make mistakes. He simply asked them to follow him—to do their best to live like him.

Just like those first followers, you don't need to be perfect to share God's love in the world. You won't always get it right, but all Jesus asks is that you follow him wholeheartedly—with ALL your heart!

"COME AND FOLLOW ME," JESUS SAID.

—— MATTHEW 4:19 ——

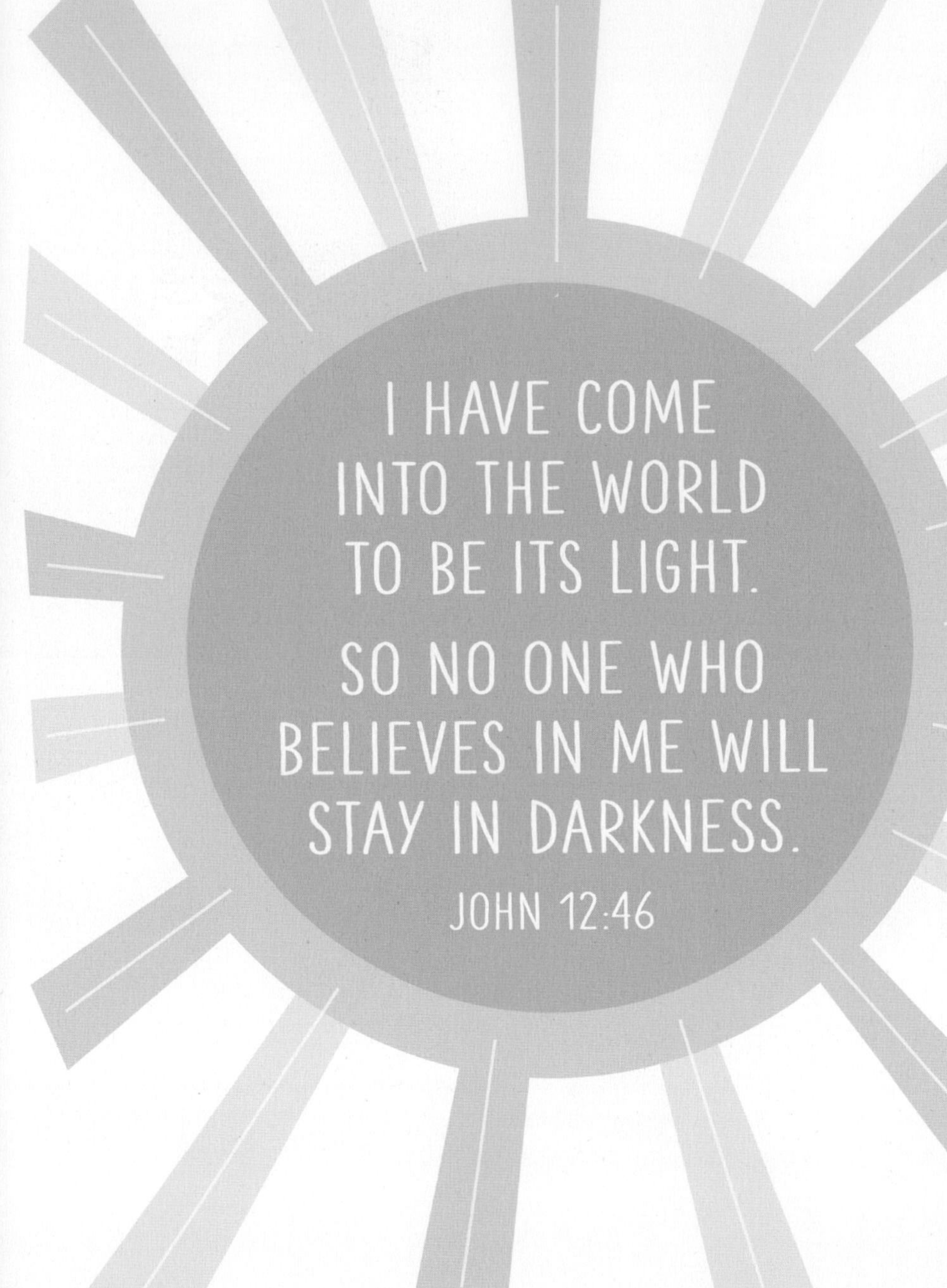
I HAVE COME
INTO THE WORLD
TO BE ITS LIGHT.
SO NO ONE WHO
BELIEVES IN ME WILL
STAY IN DARKNESS.
JOHN 12:46

NO NEED TO BOAST

To be a little light is to reflect God's light into the world and to shine it everywhere you go, doing good for others.

You don't need to shine a spotlight on yourself!

You don't need to let everyone know about the good things you do.

So there's no need to keep track of what you do for others. There's no need to make sure that someone else has noticed.

Instead, just keep loving the people around you, quietly and joyfully bringing your light to the world by finding what needs to be done and doing it.

True love doesn't boast about itself and you don't need to either.

Quietly do good deeds because it's simply the loving thing to do.

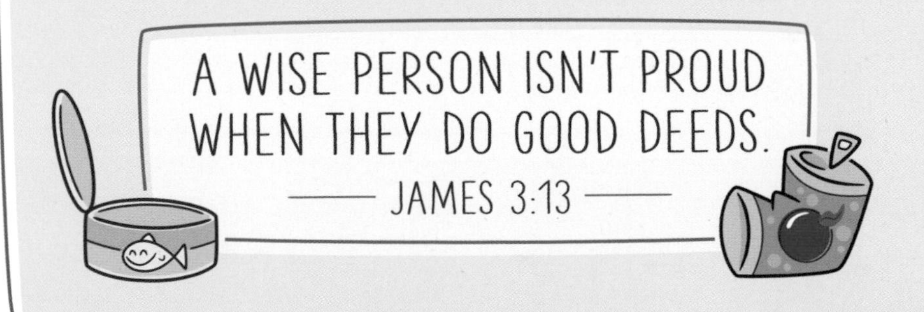

GOD IS FOR YOU

God is for you!

The God who made everything, the maker of all the heavens and everything on earth, is on your side!

When you wake up in the morning, when you go to bed at night, and when you're right in the middle of your day, God is with you, loving you and wanting the best for you.

He's quick to forgive. There's no bigger love.

There is nothing and no one stronger than him!

That means there is nothing that can separate you from his love—not sadness or difficult days, worry, mistakes, or even what other people think.

Nothing can take God's love from you.

So you never need to worry, feel alone, or afraid. You belong to God, and he is always and forever on your side.

SINCE GOD IS ON OUR SIDE, WHO CAN BE AGAINST US?

— ROMANS 8:31 —

EVERYONE HAS A STORY

Everything about you is unique. You have your own story.

We all do.

That's an important thing to remember when you find yourself in a situation where it feels difficult to be patient, forgiving, or even loving.

When you see someone who is acting angry or doing something unkind, stop and ask yourself: What might this person's story be? Why do they feel this way? What might they need?

Has someone been unkind to them? Did something sad happen? Perhaps they just need to be loved.

Maybe you can be the person to bring them God's love!

We all need patience and love from each other.

No one is less deserving of love whatever their story might be. In fact, the people Jesus spent most of his time caring for had difficult or sad stories.

So always do your best to be gentle, patient, and loving with everyone, even when it's difficult.

DON'T BE PROUD AT ALL.
BE COMPLETELY GENTLE. BE PATIENT.
PUT UP WITH ONE ANOTHER IN LOVE.

— EPHESIANS 4:2 —

SHARE THE JOY

God has given you so many different gifts and opportunities. We all have so much to be thankful for, and to share with one another.

We're made to celebrate each other's joys!

The surprising thing is that sometimes we choose not to. In fact, sometimes we feel jealous when someone else gets something we don't, or can do something we can't.

But carrying jealousy around is hard on you.

Jealousy smothers your joy, because you stop thinking about what you do have, and start focusing on what someone else has. It leaves you less thankful for what God has given you.

That means you miss out on ALL the joy there is to share.

So don't be jealous. Instead, celebrate every good thing together.

Be happy for one another, and always be thankful for all that God has given you!

LET US NOT WANT WHAT BELONGS TO OTHERS.

— GALATIANS 5:26 —

FULL OF LIFE

Our world is alive!

It's full of new life that grows, changes, and provides every day.

God made it that way! He created a world that is abundant (which means full and generous) because God's love is full and generous. He wants everything he's created to have exactly what it needs to grow and thrive.

Every day a little seed somewhere starts to push through the earth. Berries grow wild, fruit grows on trees, vegetables grow in the ground ... there's new life all around us and it never stops!

God designed a world overflowing with good things.

Everyone's needs matter to God. As a little light you can help care for what God has made and share his abundant world so that everyone has enough.

THE EARTH IS FILLED WITH THE THINGS HE HAS MADE. HE MAKES GRASS GROW FOR THE CATTLE AND PLANTS FOR PEOPLE TO TAKE CARE OF.
— PSALM 104:13–14 —

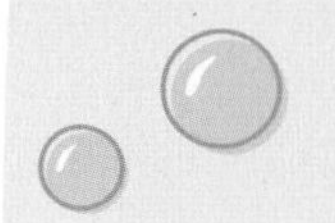

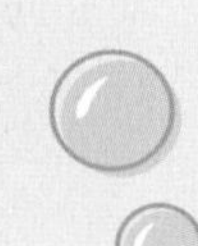

LOVE IN ACTION

More than anything, God made you to love. You're bursting with his love.

But don't just talk about it. Do something with it!

When you let it out, something amazing always happens.

When you put your love into action—when you do something loving for someone else—it comes alive!

Your love in action can bring comfort and peace. It can forgive in unexpected ways. It can offer help when someone needs it.

It encourages people. It brings light to the darkness, or hope to a difficult day.

So always be ready to jump in!

Be on the lookout for simple ways to share the love of God.

You're full of God's love, so let it show!

DEAR CHILDREN, DON'T JUST TALK ABOUT LOVE. PUT YOUR LOVE INTO ACTION. THEN IT WILL TRULY BE LOVE.

— 1 JOHN 3:18 —

THANKFUL ALL THE TIME

On happy days, when the sun is warm on your face and the birds seem especially chirpy, it's easy to be joyful! It's easy to be thankful to God because you feel glad.

On other days, though, if you're feeling sad or angry, afraid or frustrated, it's not easy to be joyful. It can be difficult to remember your reasons to thank God. We all have days when it feels harder to give thanks.

But these are really important moments because you get to practice remembering that God loves you no matter what happens, or how you feel. He is always with you.

When you remember everything that God has done for you, it helps you to stay thankful, even on the difficult days.

ALWAYS BE JOYFUL. NEVER STOP PRAYING. GIVE THANKS NO MATTER WHAT HAPPENS.

— 1 THESSALONIANS 5:16–18 —

QUICK TO LISTEN

As you go through your life, carrying your light with you, pay attention to the lights of those around you.

Just as God uses you to share his love and light with others, he can use the light of others to teach YOU new things.

There is always more to learn about yourself, about each other, and about God.

So be curious. Ask good questions. Listen to one another.

Listen to people whose stories are different from yours.

Listen to the voices of people who others might ignore. Show them they matter.

Listen when someone is sad and needs comfort. Show them they are loved and cared for.

It takes practice and patience to be a good listener. But when you listen—really listen—to someone else, you show them you care, that their story is important too.

So be quick to listen—there is always more to learn.

EVERYONE SHOULD BE QUICK TO LISTEN.
— JAMES 1:19 —

LIVE IN PEACE

Peace is the feeling you have when you are calm and relaxed, when everyone is getting along. It's how you feel when you aren't worried because you know that God is in control.

Because peace is a gift from God, you can carry it with you and share it.

When you live generously, kindly, and lovingly alongside other people, it brings peace.

When you forgive others or ask for forgiveness, that brings peace too.

When you are patient and gentle with people who are upset or angry, others can see the peace of God in you and maybe even feel it for themselves.

God made us to live together with him and with each other in harmony!

You can bring his peace with you wherever you go.

TRY YOUR BEST TO LIVE IN
PEACE WITH EVERYONE.
— HEBREWS 12:14 —

WITH ALL THAT YOU ARE

There are thousands of ways to show your love.

Jesus talked about loving God with all our hearts, all our strength, and all our minds ... with EVERYTHING that we are!

That's how God loves us!

When you use your heart, mind, and body to love God—all of your feelings, your thoughts, and your actions—there is no limit to the ways you can tell him that you love him.

Your love might have lots of words. Or none at all.

It might be noisy and full of singing or quiet and peaceful. You can tell God you love him on your own or with lots of other people. You can do it anywhere. It doesn't matter!

God has filled you with love.

Love him back with ALL that you are!

LOVE THE LORD YOUR GOD WITH ALL YOUR HEART AND WITH ALL YOUR SOUL. LOVE HIM WITH ALL YOUR STRENGTH.

— DEUTERONOMY 6:5 —

DO EVERYTHING WITH LOVE

When you have something to do, it's always up to you how you do it!

You can do your chores with a smile or with a frown. You can greet your neighbor in a grumpy way or in a glad way. You can offer help with a sigh or with a happy heart!

Choosing to do things with love (and a smile) changes you. It makes you more joyful. And it can bring joy to those around you too.

A job done gladly spreads more of God's love and light through the world.

We all have things to do—some of them are fun and some aren't. Whatever needs to be done, whether people are watching or no one sees you, do it ALL with love!

BE LOVING IN EVERYTHING YOU DO.

— 1 CORINTHIANS 16:14 —

USE YOUR VOICE

God wants our lights to be seen.

He wants our love to be visible—to be put into action.

Whenever we see something that isn't right in the world, it's our job to speak up. Especially for people who can't speak up for themselves, or whose voices can't be heard.

God cares about people who are hurt or in need. He cares about people whose needs are overlooked or whose voices are lost or ignored. He wants us to care too.

Some people are treated unfairly because of the color of their skin, where they come from, or what they don't have—money, a job, or a home.

It's up to us to use our voices and to listen to the voices of others. To make sure that everyone is heard.

That's putting God's love into action.

That's being a little light!

> SPEAK UP FOR THOSE WHO CAN'T SPEAK FOR THEMSELVES ... SPEAK UP FOR THE RIGHTS OF THOSE WHO ARE POOR AND NEEDY.
>
> — PROVERBS 31:8–9

LET YOUR
LIGHT SHINE
SO OTHERS
CAN SEE IT.
MATTHEW 5:16

SHARING IT ALL

We're all here together!

God made us to live alongside one another and share life with each other. As God's children, we are so connected to one another we can't help but be affected by each other's feelings.

If a friend or someone in our family is sad, the people around them feel that sadness.

But the amazing thing is, when we share our sadness with each other it can bring comfort and hope!

And shared joy becomes an even bigger party!

Everything is made better when we share it.

God has given you light to shine, hope to spread, comfort to offer, and joy to celebrate.

Life will always be better when we remember that we're all connected, because God made us to share everything!

IF ONE PART SUFFERS, EVERY PART SUFFERS WITH IT. IF ONE PART IS HONORED, EVERY PART SHARES IN ITS JOY.

— 1 CORINTHIANS 12:26 —

EVERY GOOD THING

God is a gift-giver! He makes things that are beautiful, things that bring us joy, make us laugh, or fill us with wonder; things that leave us speechless or full of thanks at the end of the day.

Sometimes God's gifts are small things (things that are easy to miss)—a dog's happy tail, the smell of a cake baking, a beautiful tree, or a wave from a neighbor. Sometimes his gifts are enormous, like a mountain range covered in snow, or a bright pink and red sunset.

Small or big, every good gift we have comes from God, so we can thank him for ALL the good things in our lives! Stop and look around. Keep your eyes open for God's goodness, his light and love in even the simplest things.

And the next time you feel excited or joyful, happy or full of wonder, say thank you to God because all good things come from him!

EVERY GOOD AND PERFECT GIFT IS FROM GOD.

— JAMES 1:17 —

THE SAME LOVE FOR EVERYONE

God loves each and every one of us. We are all children of God. We all belong!

God has the same love for everyone, no matter who they are, and he gives it freely.

When you remember that every person you see today, or tomorrow, or next week, is a precious child of God, it helps you to love them in that way too.

Now, everyone has a different story, and everyone has different needs. The way you show your love to one person will often be different from how you care for someone else.

But the kindness, generosity, and love you have to offer can always be the same, whoever you are with.

God loves everyone with a love that never changes. It is strong and deep. It never runs out. It is equally shared and offered to everyone.

Your love can be the same!

TREAT EVERYONE THE SAME.

— JAMES 2:1 —

JOY IN OBEDIENCE

Our hearts are made to love the things that God loves.

That means when you live the way that he wants you to live and follow his commands for your life, you find joy, because God's rules go hand in hand with his love for us.

They teach us how to forgive, which leads to peace. They teach us how to encourage and comfort one another, which brings hope.

They teach us how to put our love into action—to include everyone—which shows people what God is like (and reminds them that they are loved).

When we live this way we find ourselves closer to each other and more connected to God.

As our maker, God knows exactly what we need to thrive and grow. His rules always lead to what is best for everyone!

God shows us the way to love one another and live a life full of joy together.

DEEP INSIDE ME I FIND JOY IN GOD'S LAW.

— ROMANS 7:22 —

GOD'S ORCHESTRA

An orchestra is made up of a LOT of different instruments! Booming tubas, delicate flutes, tinkling triangles, and crashing cymbals! Of course, each instrument is wonderful on its own, but something magical happens when they all play together.

In our world, just like in an orchestra, we all have different parts to play. God has given us different gifts, and we each have something important to offer.

We need it all!

When we all play our part, listening to each other and working together, we fill the world with a light that is bigger and brighter.

So play the part that God has given you because it matters. And play it with joy!

YOU ARE THE BODY OF CHRIST.
EACH ONE OF YOU IS A PART OF IT.
— 1 CORINTHIANS 12:27 —

NEW BEGINNINGS

Have you ever noticed how much God loves new beginnings? They're all around you, in everything he's made.

Every morning the sun rises, every winter turns to spring, and whenever you ask God for his forgiveness, he gives you a fresh start because forgiveness is a new beginning too.

When you get a second chance it's a brand-new page in your story. The mistakes you have made are behind you. Tomorrow is a new day and you can try again to do your best to be a light in the world.

God wants you to be honest—to tell him when you make mistakes and to say sorry. When you do that, he will always turn those mistakes into moments for forgiveness and exciting new beginnings!

WHEN ANYONE IS IN CHRIST,
THE NEW CREATION HAS COME.
THE OLD IS GONE! THE NEW IS HERE!
— 2 CORINTHIANS 5:17 —

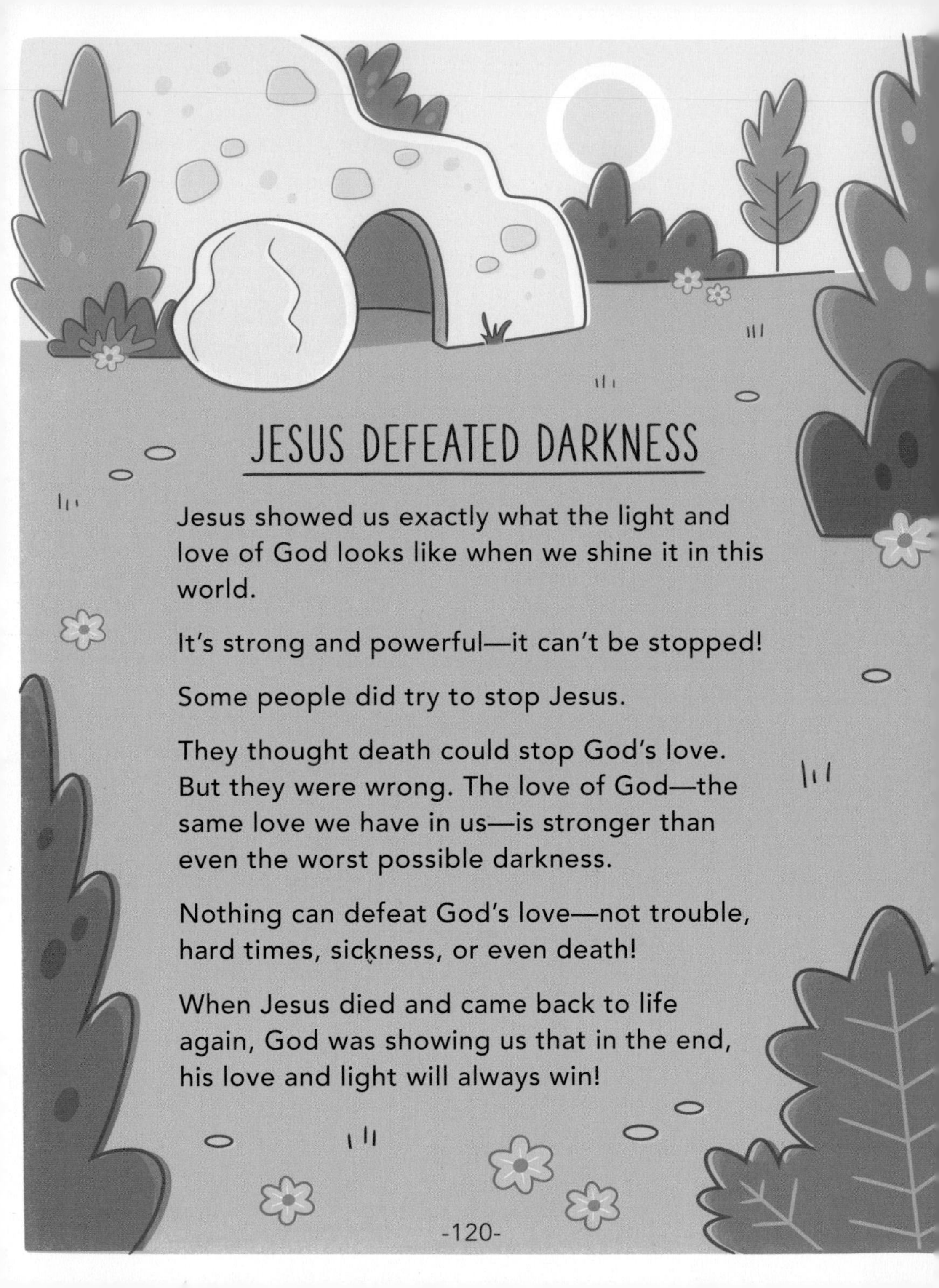

JESUS DEFEATED DARKNESS

Jesus showed us exactly what the light and love of God looks like when we shine it in this world.

It's strong and powerful—it can't be stopped!

Some people did try to stop Jesus.

They thought death could stop God's love. But they were wrong. The love of God—the same love we have in us—is stronger than even the worst possible darkness.

Nothing can defeat God's love—not trouble, hard times, sickness, or even death!

When Jesus died and came back to life again, God was showing us that in the end, his love and light will always win!

HE HAS SAVED US FROM THE
KINGDOM OF DARKNESS.
— COLOSSIANS 1:13 —

CARING FOR CREATION

God has placed us in a world he loves, to look after it. Right from the start he has asked us to help him care for creation.

It's a big, important job, and one that creates joy (like most things God asks of us) because it brings us closer to him.

When we're working outside, helping things grow and flourish, we feel more connected to God and everything he has made. That's because it's one of the things we were made to do!

We haven't always taken care of God's creation the way we were meant to. That means we have a job to do. We get to work with God, helping to fix the things that are broken, and healing the world.

So start just where you are—at home, in your neighborhood, your town, or your city. How can you look after the world around you?

We were placed into creation to care for it and love it just as God does!

THE LORD GOD PUT THE MAN IN THE GARDEN OF EDEN. HE PUT HIM THERE TO FARM ITS LAND AND TAKE CARE OF IT.

— GENESIS 2:15 —

SHARING GOD'S LOVE

God has filled you with his love.

But it doesn't stop there. It's a love that's meant to be shared.

God's love never runs out. There is always more when you give it away. And when you do, it shows others what God is like. It makes God's love visible in the world. It brings people closer to him.

It makes God's love complete!

When you share what God has given you—when you are kind, patient, forgiving, caring, and loving toward others, God's love grows and spreads in ways it never could if you just kept it for yourself.

So shine your light! Let others see the love of God in you. Show God how much you love him, by how much you love others!

NO ONE HAS EVER SEEN GOD. BUT IF WE LOVE ONE ANOTHER, GOD LIVES IN US. HIS LOVE IS MADE COMPLETE IN US.

— 1 JOHN 4:12 —

FINDING YOUR WAY

God wants you to be on a path that is good and full of life—where there is true joy!

And he shows you how to find it.

He puts people in your life who love you. You can listen and learn from their wisdom. You can read the stories of the Bible to discover more about how God wants you to live and love others. And of course you have Jesus's example to follow.

When you look for direction by doing these things, you grow closer to God, where it's easier to see what matters most to him.

Then you simply need to shine your light and share God's love in whatever you do. You'll find yourself on the right path, close to God, and full of joy.

YOU ALWAYS SHOW ME THE PATH OF LIFE. YOU WILL FILL ME WITH JOY WHEN I AM WITH YOU.
— PSALM 16:11 —

DON'T WORRY

God wants you to live a generous, thankful, and joyful life. When you're worried, that's hard to do.

Everybody worries sometimes. We worry about all sorts of things. But Jesus taught that worry doesn't add anything good to our lives—not a single thing! In fact, it can weigh you down.

God doesn't want that. He wants you to trust him because he cares for you. He knows just what you need.

When you trust God, you can tell him what you're worried about. Then you will be free to enjoy all the tremendous gifts he has given you, free to be thankful, and free to love others well.

Telling God what's on your mind always brings you closer to him. And the closer you are to him, the safer you will feel (because that's where you belong).

So whenever you're worried about something (however big or small) just bring it to God. He cares for you.

TURN ALL YOUR WORRIES OVER TO HIM. HE CARES ABOUT YOU.

— 1 PETER 5:7 —

PUTTING OTHERS FIRST

It's easy to jump to the front of the line when no one is looking—to want to be first. Or to help yourself to the biggest piece of cake so you can eat it before someone else does.

We often think that we'll be happiest when we get what we want. But the surprising and exciting truth is, God made us to feel the most joy when we're looking out for each other—when we put the needs of others ahead of our own.

When you really pay attention to the people around you and start to wonder what they might need instead of just thinking about what you want, you're truly loving people.

So take just what you need and leave the rest for others. Wait your turn, or better yet, let someone go ahead of you.

When you shine your light in that way, you might just find that there is more joy in taking care of others than there is in only thinking about yourself.

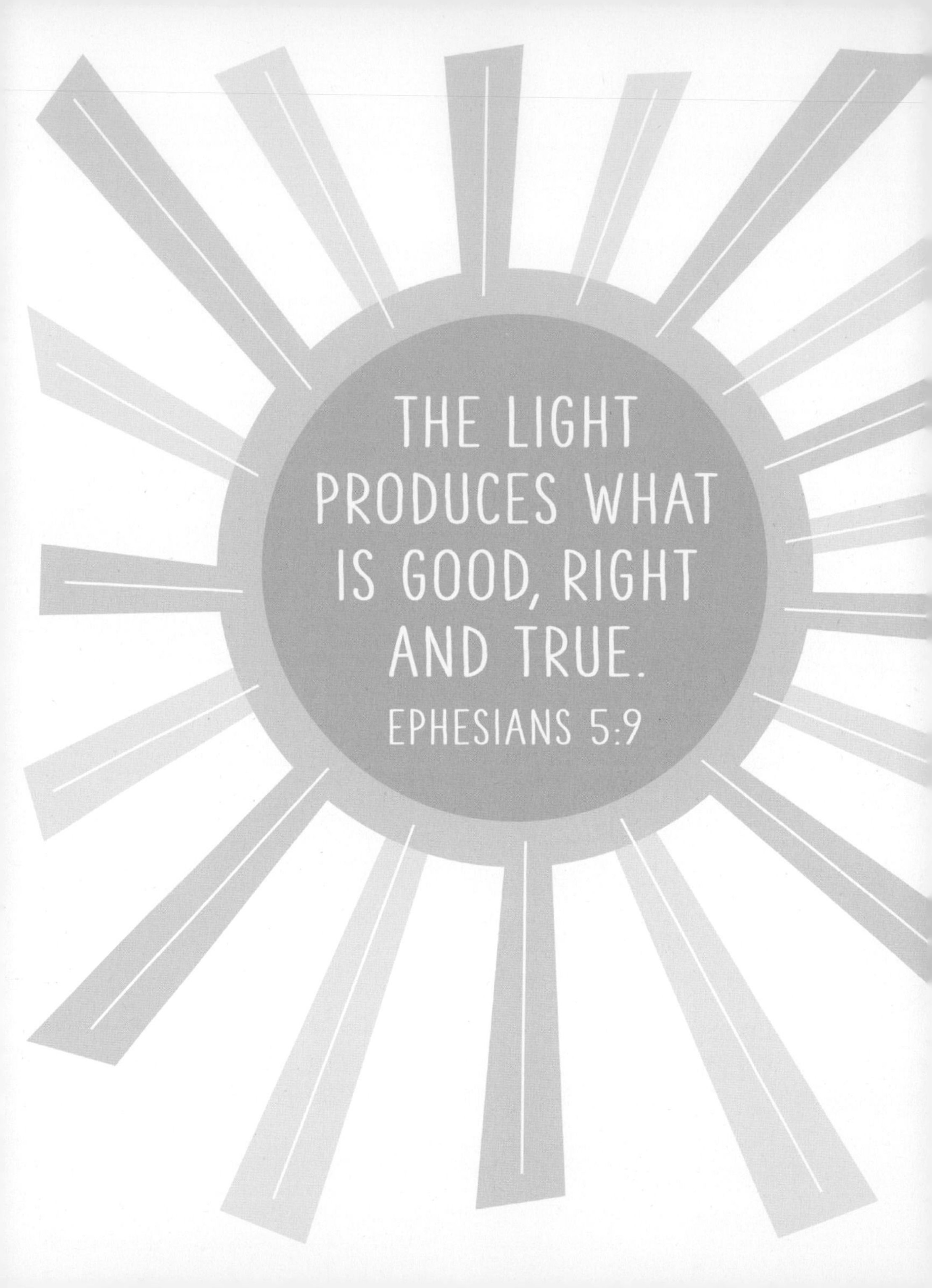
THE LIGHT
PRODUCES WHAT
IS GOOD, RIGHT
AND TRUE.
EPHESIANS 5:9

DON'T GIVE UP

Some things take time. Some things need patience.

Think about planting a seed. You dig a little hole in the ground, push the seed into the dirt, water it ... and wait.

It takes time for a plant to grow. But if you're patient and keep caring for it, eventually that little seed becomes so much more—something wonderful!

Sometimes when you shine God's light in the world and love people, especially those who need it most, you might not see the effects right away.

Sometimes people, or situations, just need a little time and a little extra care to grow into something more.

(Remember, we're all growing and learning as we go.)

So don't give up. Don't feel discouraged if things take time. Encourage each other to keep going.

Don't stop shining your light, even when no one notices or there's no prize to be won. Every bit of love you share will make the world a more loving place.

Every little bit of light you bring to the world will make it brighter for someone in the end. Sometimes it just takes time.

LET US NOT BECOME TIRED OF DOING GOOD.

— GALATIANS 6:9 —

LOVE NO MATTER WHAT

God's love doesn't need anything in return—it's given freely. God loves you unconditionally. And your love can be exactly like that.

Your job is simply to carry your light—to bring it to everyone who needs it, no matter how it's received. Sometimes people won't respond to your love the way you hope they will.

But be kind when people are mean. Be compassionate when people are angry, and gentle when people are upset.

No matter how someone responds, you can always be kind and gracious. A love like that brings peace. It shows the world that there is always another way—a loving way.

You were made to love others the way Jesus loves you—unconditionally and wholeheartedly.

LOVE ONE ANOTHER,
JUST AS I HAVE LOVED YOU.
—— JOHN 13:34 ——

BETTER TOGETHER

Sometimes beans, squash, and corn are planted very close together.

The squash's broad leaves protect the soil from the sun, the corn grows tall and supports the beans, and the beans make the soil richer. Together they all help each other grow stronger than they would be on their own.

Just like those three plants, you'll grow better when you do it with others who have different strengths—people who come from different places and have different stories from you.

God has made each of us unique! We all have different ways to encourage and build each other up. We need each other to grow well.

The more we celebrate our differences and use them to encourage and build each other up, the stronger and healthier we all grow together.

EACH OF US SHOULD PLEASE OUR NEIGHBORS. LET US DO WHAT IS GOOD FOR THEM IN ORDER TO BUILD THEM UP.

— ROMANS 15:2 —

IF YOU HAVE TWO

Sharing what God has given you is often about offering someone your time and help, your care and comfort, and of course your love. But sometimes it's simply about sharing something extra you have that someone else needs.

Sharing is something you can practice every day.

Maybe you have books you've already read, or extra cookies because you baked too many. Perhaps you have more clothes than you can wear, or toys that someone else might love!

There is SO much that you can share when you notice the extra things you have, and pay attention to what others might be missing.

It's a simple thing but it can make a huge difference.

When you share what you have, it shows people that God's love is generous!

ANYONE WHO HAS EXTRA CLOTHES SHOULD SHARE WITH THE ONE WHO HAS NONE. AND ANYONE WHO HAS EXTRA FOOD SHOULD DO THE SAME.

— LUKE 3:11 —

SHARING GOD'S COMFORT

Sometimes being a light is as simple as looking for the little ways we can comfort others—like lending your umbrella to someone on a rainy day. It's a small thing, but it makes a big difference in a storm!

We all know what it's like to be sad. When we are, God offers us his comfort. Then we get to share that same comfort with other people who need it.

If you hold someone's hand to cheer them up or give them a hug when they need one or listen when they need a friend to talk to, that's offering comfort. Even a very small kindness can make a difficult day easier.

You're never too young to bring comfort to someone who needs it.

Keep your eyes open for little ways to help!

God gives us his comfort when we need it, so that we can offer that same loving comfort to others.

HE COMFORTS US IN ALL OUR
TROUBLES. NOW WE CAN COMFORT
OTHERS WHEN THEY ARE IN TROUBLE.
—— 2 CORINTHIANS 1:4 ——

JOINED TO GOD IN LOVE

God is the creator of the universe, the source of all light and love, and he wants YOU to partner with him!

What God wants most is for everyone to know him—for the world to be as full of his love as it can possibly be.

And you get to help!

It might be something big like forgiveness. It might be something simple to help someone else.

Everything you do with God's love is something you do together with him.

So find all the ways (big and small) to live a life of love.

When you work with God to fill the world with more of his light, it doesn't just make a difference for the people around you, it brings you closer to him.

ANYONE WHO LEADS A LIFE OF LOVE IS JOINED TO GOD. AND GOD IS JOINED TO THEM.

— 1 JOHN 4:16 —

DO IT ALL WITH JOY

What do you love doing most?

Do you love growing plants, drawing pictures, or making music? Perhaps you love science or taking care of animals. Maybe you love playing games, whistling, or telling stories!

Whatever you love to do, do it all with joy!

God gave you this life and wants you to use what he has given you—your mind, your body, your skills—to live it to the fullest. You're loved and forgiven and free to find joy in so many places.

So do everything with your whole heart as a way to say thanks for all of God's gifts.

Be creative, curious, and courageous! Do everything as if you're doing it all for God. Then your joy will be hard to hide—it will light up the world.

I HAVE COME SO THEY MAY HAVE LIFE. I WANT THEM TO HAVE IT IN THE FULLEST POSSIBLE WAY.

— JOHN 10:10 —

EVERYWHERE WE LOOK

We can't see God with our eyes.

But ...

Everywhere we look, and everywhere we go, we can see what God has made.

And everything that God has made shows us something new and wonderful about who he is, because creation is full of his life, light, and love.

No matter how big or small, every little bit of creation can teach us something new about God.

We can see signs of his goodness, his creativity, his strength, his gentleness, and his love all around us.

Creation is a reflection of the one who made it!

So be curious!

Pay attention to even the smallest things that God has made.

Everything that you find along the way will be something that you discover about God.

EVER SINCE THE WORLD WAS CREATED IT HAS BEEN POSSIBLE TO SEE THE QUALITIES OF GOD ... IN WHAT HE HAS MADE.

— ROMANS 1:20 —

HOW WONDERFUL IT REALLY IS

God's love is so big!

You can only imagine how incredible it really is.

You can see it all around you, in the love of others. People shine their lights in all kinds of impossible and exciting ways.

BUT that's just a glimpse, a small reflection of God's immense love.

All of creation, everything you see, comes out of God's love. Jesus loved and forgave everyone, no matter who they were, with the love of God. And he showed that there is nothing, not even death, that can stop God's love. It always wins!

And THAT'S the love that you're connected to, the love that God has put in you, the love that you bring with you everywhere you go.

Just imagine how much you could do with THAT love!

SEE WHAT AMAZING LOVE THE FATHER HAS GIVEN US!

— 1 JOHN 3:1 —

GIVE THANKS

You have SO much to be thankful for!

There is comfort and joy in knowing you are God's child. You are loved and forgiven.

Every good thing you have comes from God—all the gifts he's given you, the people who love you, and all of creation to enjoy and care for. So say THANKS to God!

Give thanks in every way you can think of, often and with whoever happens to be around. Don't keep it to yourself.

Tell stories. Sing songs. Dance for joy.

Encourage one another by sharing all the reasons you have to be thankful and then share in the joy!

Happiness follows thankfulness. Sometimes when you're feeling down, the best solution is to find something you're thankful for. And there is always something.

So never stop giving thanks. Thank God for everything!

ALWAYS GIVE THANKS TO GOD ...
FOR EVERYTHING.
— EPHESIANS 5:20 —

WITH GOD'S HELP

God wants the world to be absolutely bursting with his love—as full as it can possibly be!

You are part of his plan to light up the world with that love, and to bring everyone closer to him, because you are a little light.

God is working in you to guide you toward all the thoughts, words, and actions that please him.

He is shaping you into the person he created you to be.

When you love God and listen to him, little by little you'll start to see more ways to be kind, helpful, and loving toward others.

With God's help you can live your whole life as a little light, connected to his great plan to show everyone his love.

GOD IS WORKING IN YOU.
HE WANTS YOUR PLANS AND YOUR ACTS TO FULFILL HIS GOOD PURPOSE.

— PHILIPPIANS 2:13 —